Spin:

Tales from the Diamond

poems by

J. R. Thelín

Finishing Line Press
Georgetown, Kentucky

Spin:

Tales from the Diamond

ACKNOWLEDGMENTS

Evening Street Review: "The Dodgers in Six"

Publisher: Leah Huete de Maines
Editor: Christen Kincaid
Cover Art: Public Domain, CC0 1.0
Author Photo: Harold J. Thelín
Cover Design: Elizabeth Maines McCleavy

Order online: www.finishinglinepress.com
also available on amazon.com

Author inquiries and mail orders:
Finishing Line Press
PO Box 1626
Georgetown, Kentucky 40324
USA

Contents

For Terri,
My First Listener

…go be a king in a field of weeds….
(Michael Ryan, "God Hunger")

Hot Dogs

His father haunts his dreams.
So does his dog. Aren't they both dead?
He wonders as they show up
for the third time this night.

His father spins a spatula
like a hot shot TV chef.
The dog waits, alert, a mist
of saliva forming at her lips.

In real life, his father barely knew
how to turn on a burner.
Suddenly he's Emeril, knives flashing
as the studio audience oohs, then applauds.

In his dream he dreams
of Saturdays at Wrigley Field.
No dogs allowed, but his father hails
a hot dog vendor who slathers on

mustard, the same brand they store
in the pantry cabinet at home,
but at the park, outdoors,
it somehow all tastes better,

more tart, more alive, with flavor.
His father stops spinning
and asks, *What you want*
on your dog, Sport? The dog rolls over,

displays the pink underside
of her belly. They all sit down for dinner,
make a small blessing that includes the Cubs
winning their first pennant since 1945.

Night Game in the Midwest

Mosquitoes flutter and dive
under the only light, an ancient lamp
hung at a corner in the park
as the next batter stamps
his feet at the makeshift home plate,
a battered pizza box
that's seen better days.

The scuffed up softball
can barely be seen
especially if hit to deep
center where Little Joey floats
like a ballet dancer,
his glove invisible in the dark.

The night's silence unfolds
around us, covers up
a rare crack of the bat
as Fast Eddie legs it to second
on a hit that would have been
an easy out in daylight.

Our mothers know better
than to call us in. We love the spin
of the ball, whether visible or not.
The game is endless and quiet
as we lace up sneakers night after night.

Midwest Twister

That smell.
The air heavy yet brittle
with tornado odor.

A brooding quiet
as if an angry god
was deciding
which sinners to strike down next

                      in vengeance,
                      in glory.

Far, but not too far.
We could see the black whirlwind
and wondered
if a wicked witch
would be bound to a broomstick in its center
whirling and wailing.

Pick-up game
suddenly ended;
a Louisville Slugger bat once choked up
let loose and rolling toward third.

Our playground
an open, naked target
as the sprint toward our homes began,

heels and toes kicking up,
sneakers learning to fly.

'Take Your Cut'

I heard the rifle crack of the bat
as I lined a surprise double
over the second baseman's head.
Hitting .138, I posed no threat

to opposing pitchers who glared
down at me from dandelion-covered
mounds. Kept in the lineup
because of my glove that gobbled up

bad hoppers and screaming drives
the outfield never saw, I brought
my fear to home plate, that piece
of ash bearing down on my shoulder

before I took a few practice cuts
then trembled into a batter's stance.
But today, perched on second,
ready to sprint to third, I felt

like I'd joined the club at last,
felt veins in my arms burst with pride.

Diamonds Are a Boy's Best Friend

I was smooth at second,
my "Little Looie" Aparicio mitt magnetic,

attracting hot grounders and line drives
to center, slap zap slap hardballs

with smeared seams would be
welcomed by me, my glove,

and the love I shared with teammates
and opponents on dusty, rocky

diamonds all across that Midwest city,
the sun naked and fiery in a summer sky.

Tools of the Trade (Pickup Games on Our Block)

We use whatever is at hand
for bases: crinkly pie plates; pizza boxes
flecked with bits of stale cheese;
a frisbee Jimmy's beagle took
a bite out of. Our games, legendary, last for weeks
so we choose Crazy Eddie to scavenge
for replacements ripe for further damage.

The Dodgers in Six

I think I was the only one
in my fourth-grade class
who rooted for the Dodgers—
newly transplanted to L.A.—
in the '59 World Series
duking it out (oh, Duke Snider
in left) with the Chi-Sox

while we watched the game
on a black & white TV <u>in class</u> (!)
at Charles Gates Dawes Elementary School,
440 Dodge Avenue in Evanston,
a suburb that bordered Chicago
on the north and lest we forget

Dawes served as V-P
for Cal Coolidge, a nowhere president
if ever there was one but who
probably would have cheered on
the Sox even after slugger Ted Kluszewski
sat down on third base and wept.

To Hell With Heroes

I'll scoop up my early spring collection
of baseball cards, leave you splayed on the grass

wondering why I would not trade you
for a Ron Piché or an Ernie Broglio,

their arms seizing up and sent back
to the disabled list, another asterisk

on their records, their diminishing stats,
an omen, a warning that few last

in the majors, the minors are for up
'n' comers or losers who can't face

years in sporting goods departments
trying to hawk signature gloves

to kids like us before the stars
in our eyes dim, then blink out

Cubs

My flannel PJs are crusty
from spitting up on them in sleep.
My face and arms are crusty
from the onslaught of chicken pox.
The voices are crusty with static
as I try to tune to a station in Memphis.

During this week in bed I lay out
Topps baseball cards, making up
the Chicago Cubs lineup, better
than their actual manager, Bob
"Why Win When You Can Lose" Scheffing,
or that's what my dad calls him.

And he calls them like he sees them,
especially when he's behind home plate
as a volunteer ump for my Cub Scout softball league,
a pitiful group of 5th graders who dream
of kicking up chalk dust
when sliding safely into third at Wrigley Field.

Sacrificed

Sick on my birthday, I huddled
under a homemade afghan
on the living room couch. My father,

recently arrived from his daily commute,
tossed me 1-2-3 packs of baseball cards.
I'd been expecting a box.

I'd have given the Double Bubble
flat rectangles of pink gum
to Jeff Weinberg, always chewing a wad

like Don Zimmer at Wrigley Field,
the occasional spit of brown gunk
at the third base bag as he squatted,

a mini-behemoth ready to pounce
to gobble up a wicked grounder
or a sacrifice bunt or take

a line drive in his massive chest.
Dad gave a low chuckle after each pack
he chucked my way. I thought it would serve

him right if I learned how to stuff
chewing tobacco in my mouth, my cheek
rotting away before I was old enough to vote.

My Childhood List of Possessions (Part 3)

I had solitary baseball games
pounded against the back wall
of our small brick house, the sound inside
a fusillade of bombs
going off for hours at a time.

I had baseball cards
I whispered to at night
as the AM transistor radio
murmured talk shows next to my right ear lobe.
The players, like the O'Brien brothers
on the Pirates, became my close friends
though Johnny and Eddie O. never became
more than utility infielders
or occasional relief pitchers,
trying anything, or so I believed,
to remain Big Leaguers.

Beleaguered by mumps, measles, and chicken pox,
I had days and nights of hallucinatory
pro-ball games and radio announcers,
covered in calamine lotion. Before drifting
into the sweet narcosis of sleep,
I'd track the hushed intimacy
of late night talk radio,
conversation rising like steam from a thick mug
of hot chocolate just about to cool.

I had cool sheets
that met my recently showered body.
I was clean and ready for the true world
of dreams, baseball cards resting
between thumb and forefinger,
Linda Darnell reflecting on Tyrone Power,
how the present never matched the past,
how the future was all I really had.

I Tell You, Baseball is a Spiritual Game

I learned to meditate in right field,
my choice, no one else wanted
to play there, but I inhaled
sweet clover and recently mowed
bluegrass by the school's facilities'
crew, several men who listened
to WGN-Radio on lunch breaks,
the Cubs pre-game shows, all

insane hope that *this* year they'd rise
from the cellar, homeruns flying
over the ivy growing
into the center field wall, kids
like me hanging in space, gloves
in place for the first dinger of the season.

Practice Makes Perfect

He threw me grounders
until the light faded out,
our lawn bumpy with bits
of rock and built-up ant hills.

As soon as I was nine,
I tried out for Little League,
the only third grader on the field.
I fielded every ball hit to me

at second base, a smile and a nod
from a coach or two, *but he's too
small, too young, our nine year olds
have already been scouted,*

*already selected, no place
on any team for him. Next year,
maybe next year,* so I signed up
for Farm League where any fool

with a glove was accepted,
and my father started hurling harder,
with greater heat, making me dive and leap
for that little white pill,

my arms growing more and more elastic
with each liner or grounder I speared
or gobbled up like the only meal ever eaten.

Another Game Called Because of Tornado

That funnel cloud
ripped up
our school
backdrop
lifted it
for blocks
then spit it out
in Jo-Jo's
backyard
metal mangled
a surreal
sculpture
we hated to see
the city
haul
to the dump
now a pit stop
for migrating
birds
who know
nothing at all
about baseball

Play at the Plate

Even in my itch-inducing woolens,
I stretched before a game, my legs
taut with the idea, the memory
of sliding into home, cleats
exploding with dust and old clods
of dirt, the hapless reach
of the catcher who could not
tag me out. Was there any doubt?
Plenty. I had stumbled at the bag
rounding third as I heard the cry
of the pitcher who directed
the center fielder to hurl that pill
to the plate, catcher's mitt
and umpire waiting, as if all
motion had stopped, if only
for the moment when I started
my slide, teeth gritted, limbs tensed,
before I became a bomb captured
by some parent's camera lens.

New Kid

He took his fungo bat
and tripped me, sent me
flying until playground
asphalt dug into my knees.
I could feel blood seep
into my pants, new ones
bought at K-Mart, they, like me,
unlikely to last the first season
at school, a new school,
a move to the suburbs,
trading in stickball on the streets
for tangle of tetherball stuck
on a pole near manicured
lawns, the constant swish-swish
of sprinklers wasting water
like we'd never do in the city,
and I'd thrash that dude
till he wailed, and peeled home
to mama, but the old lady warned me
with her fist, *behave Rocky,*
or your butt will be sore for a month,
so I guess I can stand
scraped knees for a week.

Cowboys to Girls

Why were all the uniforms so scratchy?
Little League Pony League it didn't matter

I'll take Farm League any day no
jerseys or pants only caps better than

nothing I guess I'd be thrilled just
to make contact bat against ball a hit

or an out it didn't matter like dating
in high school the ask was all-important

not so much the result his teachers
kept giving him detention he kept

cutting up in class and we couldn't
help ourselves we had to laugh

My Oh So Brief High School Freshman Baseball Career

Picked off first again,
the only player
never to suit up for games.

A Talk with Wolfgang and Ernie in Black & White

He did not look
like a boy who loved
opera, decked out
in jeans and checked shirt,
his work boot pushing down
on a spade on his family's
weedy lawn, one of his summer
chores to help pay for

the ten-speed of his dreams.
He looked like Any Kid USA,
not one who knew the score—
and libretto—inside out of *Don Giovanni*,
considered Mozart a mentor
as much as Ernie Banks
of the Chicago Cubs. After the photo
snapped by his father, he rubs

his hands full of dirt as if he were
up next in the batter's box, wonders
who's on the mound today
against The Phillies who always
seem to beat the Cubbies
even at home, even as he belts out
a *DG* passage, his arms conducting
that last thrilling crescendo....

Historical Racism

I pour through a baseball guide, players' names and statistics looking back in the 1800s. The stats tell so little, really, though that's all most readers and fans can recall. What if we could open a flap and walk around in the fabric of their lives? The statistics say so little. Take Satchel Paige, who some say was the greatest hurler of all time. But the guide only reveals his record in the show, not his staggering stats in the Negro Leagues, confined

to one small slice of America, like the last piece of diner peach pie in a tin that goes stale, then is thrown out

Stealing Home

On the burned out scraggle of a diamond
far from the playground chatter and hopscotch markers,
we sixth graders, a self-selected but scruffy group,
chalked our hands and planned our strategies
under the looming eye of nearby Mount Trashmore,
a wild and benevolent god we loved but feared
to climb. What other elementary school owned
such a wonder? It would guide us
to victory over other pickup teams our age

butting up against our district
but a world away with few Weinbergs or Rubins
or Feinsteins. Daredevil Jews. They flew
down base paths headfirst, couldn't resist
stealing second, third, home plate, tucking them
neatly in the crease of Negro or goyim
signature gloves. We loved each other back then.
Or say, at least, we loved being together—scuffling infield dirt
or floating on the weedy outfield turf.

We made the rules. We called the shots.
We sacrificed bunts—and ourselves, gently yanking
a flailing hurler, like me, after the first inning
knowing this was best for us all.
By Pony League, though, Jeff Weinberg suited up
in his scratchy woolen Richard Allen Ball Bearings uniform
steam-ironed to perfection by his mother, Miriam.
As I, in my Evanston Sand & Gravel pinstripe red,
hung him a bad hook, I could see something click off

in Jeff's eyes as he dragged a spinning bunt
down third. My Jewish friends
began to turn away. They sent me no invitations
to bar mitzvahs. With one exception:
At Mark Coleman's Bar Mitzvah, Miriam Weinberg cruised by me
as if I were no more than an errant leaf

hugging, momentarily, the bag at third base
and she, having knocked one out of the park,
smiled and coasted home.

Our Town

Too many houses squat
like a dog staked and forgotten,
blinds always closed, hanging,
a flag no one will unfurl again.

Anybody home? the town drunk
slams his fist against a screen door.
Maybe he will find a way in,
curl by a fireplace, try to imagine

heat from a handful of ashes
scattered like selective memories,
his wife fixing him Eggs Benedict,
his favorite, his son begging him

for a game of catch before twilight
descends, before they scrunch up
together in front of the old Philco radio,
a local announcer barking out

play-by-play action they can almost see,
a hard line drive to center, the slide
headfirst into third, and endless
cheers from seats deep in the bleachers.

Why I Hate Professional Sports

President Harding died I imagine
in a worn-to-his-body-shape
armchair cigar smoldering
in a nearby ashtray a quiet
solemn affair hardly noticed
by anyone like and unlike
my uncle Max who blew out
his brains on Lake Michigan
after he rowed out to a calm secluded place
his arms muscular ropes
that fake punched me as we sparred
in his garage he always let me win
in the end a photo of Joe Louis pinned
to the wall above a vise he used
to saw 2x4's wood dust
flying up my nose Lou Boudreau on the AM
providing colorful commentary
on the Cubs even in their dark
days of the '50s and early '60s
GM John Holland having traded
away their best young players for unfortunate
stiffs like George Altman and Ernie Broglio.

1984

At 34 I purchased my first
brand new TV a Sharp
The Cubs were in their first
playoff in forever a fan
since I was five I was
glued to the set with its awesome
visuals I could spy the moles
on Andre Dawson's face in left
and the scuff of dirt Ryne
Sandberg kicked up at second

but I got so worked up
I couldn't sit or stand still
limbs launching into a tarantella
I tell you the only
thing I could do was turn
off the set and start a series
of pranayama breaths
that lasted until I read
the Astros had shut
Chicago down again.

Post-MFA Summer Conference

Syd Lea bellows the blues
in the student center basement
while Bruce Weigl shang-a-langs
under an intermittent strobe light
someone dug out from a hall closet
discovered behind a set of janitor's mops

we make do with what we've got
no es verdad? I hope Syd steers clear
of anything Español though "Wooly
Bully"—uno dos tres quatro—would be
acceptable tomorrow there's a softball
game scheduled poets against the fiction

writers you can guess who has the speed
and who sports the heavy hitters
last year Rivard slid into home
skinned his knee while safe at the plate
his Grand Canyon grin lit up the entire diamond.

Semi-Pro Instructional Guide to Hitting, Lesson on Psychology, #3

Plant your feet firmly
in the box, sway with a cool
heat toward your enemy,
the pitcher, who will use
any means to connive you
into whiffing at an imaginary

target. Emery board, spit, K-Y Jelly,
even good old elbow grease
is allowed. Captain Doom on the mound,
he glares down at you from his elevated
position 60 feet away. You will not
confuse him with your 2nd grade

teacher, the Witch of Hazlehurst Elementary,
who clamped her cold scaley fingers
on your left ear, dragged you
whimpering to the even colder
office of the principal, Dr. Nichol ("he's a pickle,"
you'd chorus). No. Do not confuse the tunnel

from the locker room to the dugout
with the waxed halls of Hazlehurst. Instead,
imagine that pathetic pill-thrower as a video game
monster, and your lightning response
will batter the seamed white light
back at him, tear his mitt

off—or better yet, his head—until
the one who looked down at you loses all
sense of his own rhythm, discovers
ticks and jerks in the once-smooth delivery
of arm, hand, eye, and ball. He will
now aim, not throw, a dead man on the hill.

Pitching 101

Greg Maddux seems completely
in control on the mound and I don't know
how he does it his speed is not remarkable
but the ball is always hopping as if
he zapped it with an electrical charge
I remember how I thought
I put nothing on the softball
in sixth grade I just put it
over the plate in a slow drooping arc
that left batters flailing at the wind
it should have been so easy to hit
I'll bet they and I were both
assuming a big thought balloon over
our collective heads and there goes
Maddux again another whiff
another K marked on the scorecard I so enjoy
filling in with non-erasable ink.

Out at the Plate

We're trapped inside the Kingdome.
Nell buys junk food *because it's there, and we're here.*
Hard balls bounce on Astroturf like God never intended.
Mike recites a poem from memory, but I can't concentrate
on his voice, only on the rumble of static from a loudspeaker
announcing the next batter, a cast-off from a team even worse
than The Mariners, fighting not to fall deeper into the cellar.
My skin, normally moist and healthy in the Pacific-Northwest climate,
starts to itch. We're stuck in the bleachers, and I want to reach
for a foamy brew slopping over the rim of a plastic cup, but I don't
    drink
anymore and I might capsize at any moment—when the crack of a bat
wakes me, and I am forced out at second base *again*, the runner at first
giving me the *I'm sorry* sign. I will never steal home at this rate.

Flashing the Leather

I purchased that mitt to play catch
with her son at a nearby park
or on the asphalt at the side
of Dick's Sporting Goods on South Academy,
the slap of ball against glove
drowned out by the drone of engines
humming and sputtering. I bought it
at Dick's, swabbed neatsfoot oil
into its leather, wrapped it
with two balls to keep its shape.

It's been years since I threw one
of those spherical bodies, and if
I did now, my right arm would probably fall off,
that's how old I really am
even though I curl free weights
and use stretch bands to ease the pain
in my failing rotator cuffs,
but I still remember that impossible
catch I made in Little League,
a screaming liner speared on the hot corner
that left the opposing team's coach at third
gasp in wonder
and appreciation, I'd like to think.

Spin

She put spin on the ball;
        and her son didn't like it
                at all. Still, at seven, I could tell

he was thrilled to chase his mother
        on and off the base paths, risk
                being called sissy by his cocksure buddies.

Strike three. Strike four. What did it
        matter, how many? their time together
                was "no time." Real time. As he dug in,

his imaginary spikes gripping the earth,
        his eyes piercing her heart before each swing.
                She hadn't played since her tomboy years;

but her strut-around-the-mound and her chatter
        that cracked him up so that he'd whiff at her
                balloon ball and fall down on home plate,

made him moan when she hollered, "Game's over!"
        My father taught me spin, English
                he called it, on the ping pong table

in Joel Margulies' garage. It seemed
        unfair, a ball dipping and looping
                and sliding that much. How could he chop

down like that *without* missing? In truth,
        his paddle stroked more air than ball.
                That was the secret. Becoming the current of air

let that little plastic-coated spheroid
        tumble and dive like spray above incoming waves.
                At first, I hated his laugh, almost as crooked

as his serves. But after a summer's practice,
        slowly skunking my peers, I felt the swerve
                come into my own wrist.

Tonight I delight in watching you
        and your son. Pick-up sticks. Pre-video game,
                for sure, but still going strong on your kitchen table.

This is a game between the two of you;
        I'm just the lucky voyeur, careful
                not to disturb...as Gavin lifts a red plastic

stick, so patiently, so gently, as if
        he were delivering the one microbe that could save
                the world. It does. So he gets to flip

the next stick—a rule unknown to me so I assume
        it's a Marianne & Gavin variation confined
                to this kitchen—and it leaps over the lip

of the table, dashed and dazzled on the floor
        like a little Nijinsky. I could dance
                my own ballet right now but remain quiet,

a big stupid smile on my face, a new memory
        tucked away in my hip pocket.
                Later, Gavin will ring you on your second line;

and you'll fly upstairs to tuck him in,
        call "love you" back and forth like a match
                that never ends, never reveals winner or loser.

We'll scrunch up together on your love seat,
        and while I rub your feet, you'll relate
                how your mother died sitting up

at her kitchen table, stirring her coffee
content to leave her body in that sacred place.
She taught me about being still and loving,

you'll say, *never an unkind word passed her lips.*
I'll say, *My father—also dead—taught me about spin
and I'm ready to listen to the spin of our memories.*

J. R. Thelín is the author of three previous poetry chapbooks: *Those Last Few Moments of Light: Poems of the Dead Boy* (Slipstream Press, 2023); *The Way Out West* (2005, Concrete Wolf) and *Dorrance, Narrative, History* (2004, Pudding House Publications), as well as two full-length collections, *Last Cha Cha in Albuquerque* (2017, Main Street Rag Press) and *Breath Into Bone* (2010, Small's Books). He has served as co-coordinating editor of *the eleventh MUSE* and as poetry reader for *Shenandoah*. After working for many years in Development, including stints at Colorado College and Washington and Lee University, Thelín retired as senior development researcher from University of Virginia at the end of 2020. A graduate of Colorado College (B.A.) and Vermont College of Fine Arts (M.F.A.), he is married and lives, writes, and walks in Buena Vista VA.

*9 7 9 8 8 9 9 9 0 0 7 6 1 *